Plurry
a scheme for a musical instrument

Guy Ottewell

Copyright © 1998, 2009, 2019 by Guy Ottewell
First printing November 1988
2nd printing August 1992
2nd edition, November 2009
3rd edition, May 2019

ISBN 978-0-934546-77-5

Universal Workshop
www.UniversalWorkshop.com
Greenville, S.C., U.S.A., and Lyme Regis, Dorset, England

4 Basic description

6 Plures

13 Uses of plures

15 Sets

18 The pattern of playing

21 Shifts

23 Theory

26 F Lydian

27 Structural order—fucigidaeb

29 Intervals

31 Transformation I: musics based on other numbers

32 Transformation II: from natural to well-tempered scale

32 Transformation III: the plurry-pattern otherwise applied

36 Afternote

Introduction

Plurry is my name for a musical instrument which does not yet exist, and may never exist, yet the contemplation of ir can reveal and clarify much about the mathematical basis of music.

The distinguishing aspect of the plurry is not the material of which it is made, nor the mechanism by which its tones are produced (there could be various such mechanisms), but the spatial arrangement of the tones. They are arranged not along one dimension but along two.

If actually built, a plurry would of course make easier the visualization of what it reveals about the structure of music: it could be a teaching tool. It might also have some merits for the player. Certain tone-series, which I call plures, would be played on it with simple actions; and the actions for playing in all keys would be the same.

4

Plurry is my name for a musical instrument which does not yet exist, and which may never exist, yet the contemplation of which can reveal and clarify much about the mathematical basis of music.

The distinguishing aspect of the plurry is not the material of which it is made, nor the mechanism by which its tones are produced (there could be various such mechanisms), but the spatial arrangement of the tones. They are arranged not along one dimension but along two.

If actually built, a plurry would of course make easier the visualization of what it reveals about the structure of music: it could be a teaching tool. It might also have some merits for the player. Certain tone-series, which I call plures, would be played on it with simple actions; and the actions for playing in all keys would be the same.

Basic description

Let us assume that the generators of sound are strings, represented by the vertical lines on the diagram. (As we shall see later, they could instead be bars, tubes, or something else.)

The strings are stretched on a sounding-board. They are divided into sub-strings by bridges, represented on the diagram by short horizontal marks.

The strings are of alternate colors, say green and red, represented in our diagram by double and single lines.

The strings are "ideal" ones, of equal composition and at equal tension. Therefore the pitch sounded by each sub-string is in exact inverse proportion to its length: the longer the sub-string, the lower its pitch.

Each sub-string is 2 times as long as the sub-string immediately above it. Therefore it sounds 1/2 as high; that is, an octave lower. For example, if one sub-string of any string sounds F, then the next sub-string below it sounds F an octave below. All the other sub-strings of that string sound F in different octaves.

While the factor between sub-strings of a string is 2, the factor between adjacent strings is 3. Each sub-string is 3 times as long as one of the sub-strings on the string immediately to the right of it. Therefore it sounds 1/3 as high, that is, a musical twelfth lower. It follows that it is 3/2, 3/4, 3/8, etc., times as long as other sub-strings of that string, and therefore sounds 2/3, 4/3, 8/3, etc., times as high; that is, a fifth lower, a fourth higher, an eleventh higher, etc. Thus if the sub-strings of one string sound F in different octaves, then all the sub-strings of the next string to its right sound C in different octaves.

The sub-strings are arranged on the board at heights corresponding to their pitch: each sub-string lies higher on the board than all sub-strings sounding lower than it. For example each sub-string sounding an F lies slightly higher than the nearest E and slightly lower than the nearest E♯.*

---

* The diagram is plotted with the sub-strings in their true relative positions. It turns out that the formula for the vertical position of a given sub-string, as measured from the position of the lowest sub-string shown, is that it is 2 times the length of that lowest sub-string minus 2 times the sub-string's own length. Since the sub-strings continually diminish in length upward, they approach and never reach a limiting line across the diagram, at 2 times the length of *any* sub-string. In other words, if you measure from the bottom of any sub-string to its top, and then an equal distance upward, you will come to this invisible limiting line, which represents a length of zero and a frequency of infinity.

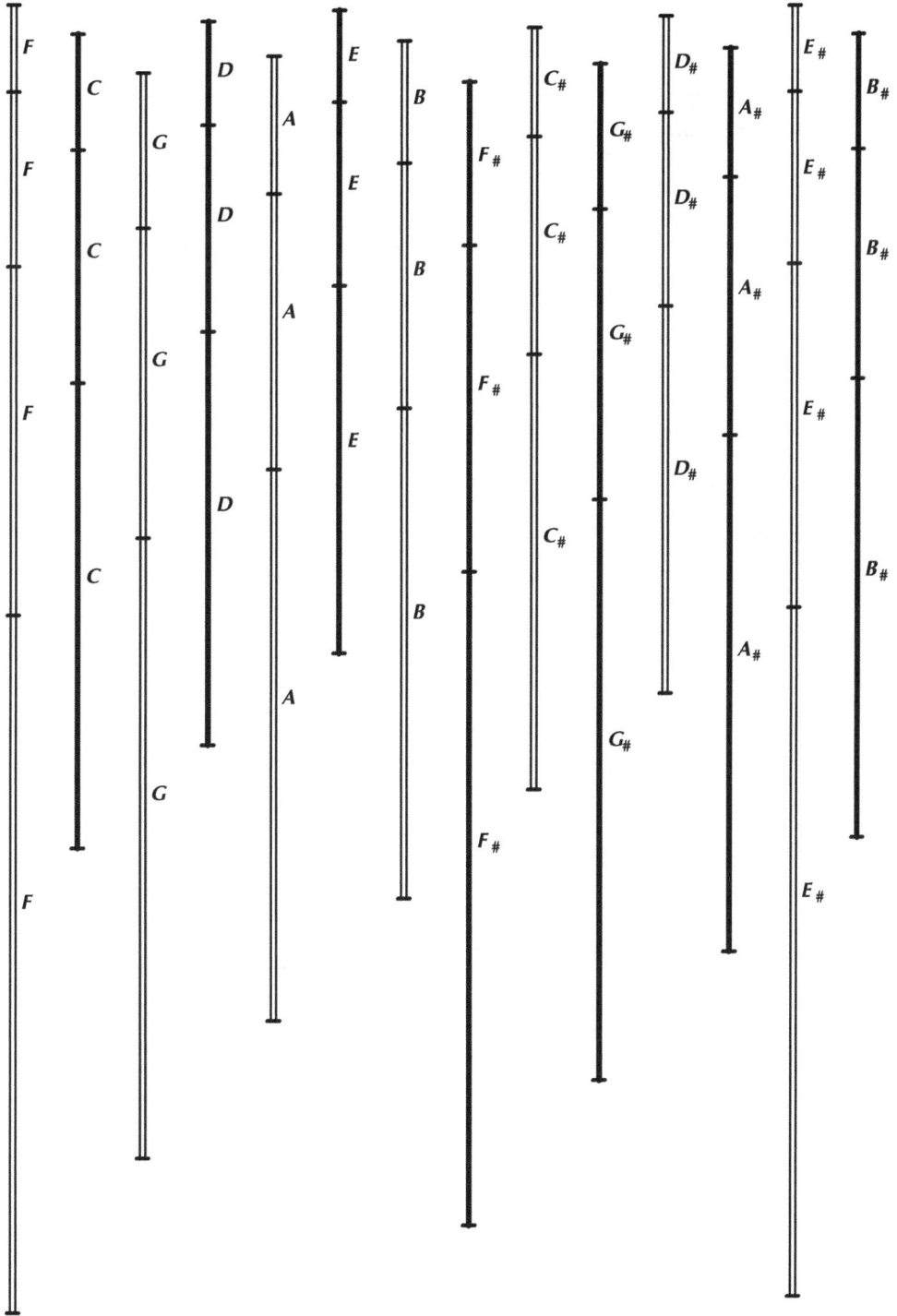

6

The letter-names of the tones may be marked on the board beside or under the strings. It will be convenient to think of the positions of the letters as representing the positions of the tones, and to imagine usually striking the strings at these points.

Any tuning of the strings may be used. If the leftmost string is F as shown, then the others will automatically be as shown: C G D A E B F♯ C♯ G♯ D♯ A♯ E♯ B♯. If the leftmost string were to be C, the others would be G D A E B F♯ C♯ G♯ D♯ A♯ E♯ B♯ F𝄪; if B♭, then F C G D A E B F♯ C♯ G♯ D♯ A♯ E♯; if F♭, then C♭ G♭ D♭ A♭ E♭ B♭ F C G D A E B; if F♭♭, then C♭♭ G♭♭ D♭♭ A♭♭ E♭♭ B♭♭ F♭ C♭ G♭ D♭ A♭ E♭ B♭.

We have shown sub-strings to each string within a range of 4 octaves, but the range could obviously be extended by adding higher (shorter) and lower (longer) sub-strings.

What is less obvious from our experience with other instruments is that the range could also be extended laterally. We have shown 14 strings, but we could add more to left and right. B♭♭ and other flats and even double-flats could be added to the left, and F𝄪 and other double-sharps could be added to the right.*

Plures

A plure is a series of tones lying along one line on the plurry, so that all the tones can be played with a single sweep of the finger (or plectrum).

Since the lines are all curves which are convex upward, they are suited to the radial movements of the player's arms. Plures of this form will most often be played by the left hand (in either direction):

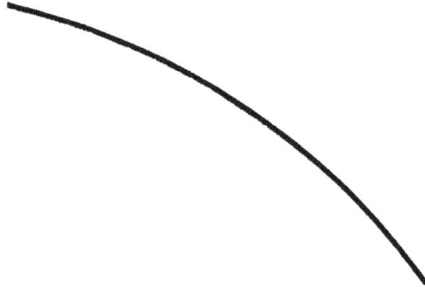

plures of this form by the right:

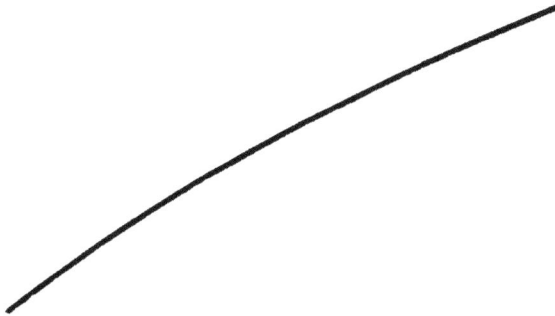

---

* The traditional sign for double sharp is 𝄪. But this cannot be extended if we want to talk about theoretical treble sharps etc.

Plures of fifths are steep right-hand plures. For example:

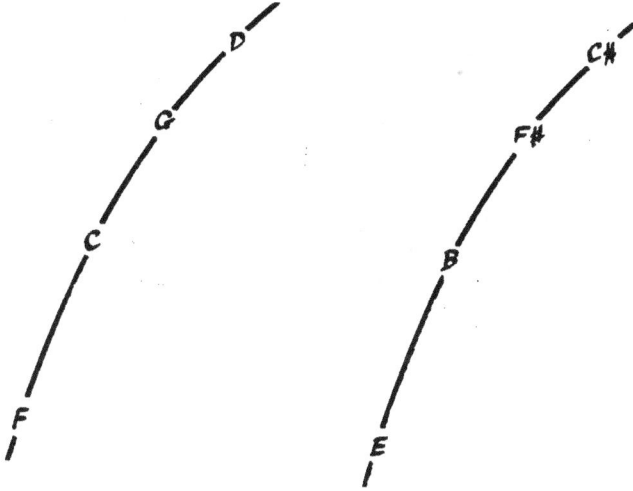

Plures of fourths are left-hand plures, not quite so steep:

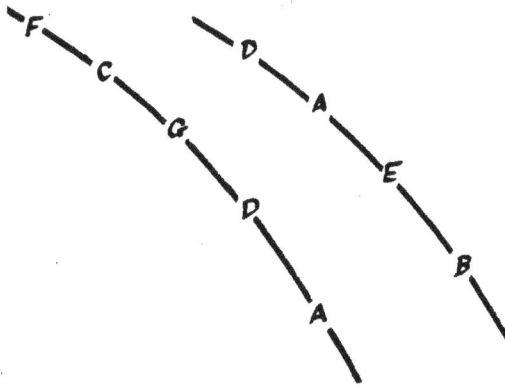

Plures of fourths and fifths are gently sloping right-hand plures. They travel either above a line of red bridges and below a line of green ones:

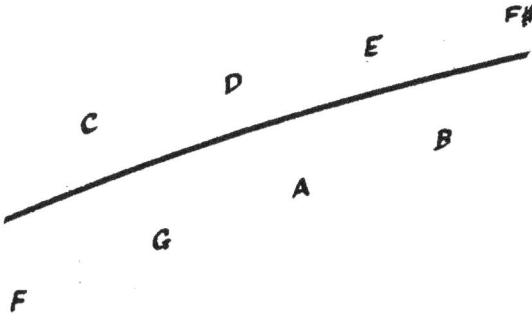

or above a line of green bridges and below a line of red ones:

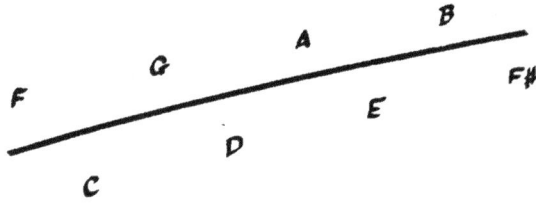

Played from left to right, they sound as alternate downward fourths and upward fifths; from right to left, upward fourths and downward fifths.

Plures of whole-steps (seconds) travel parallel to plures of fourths-and-fifths, but along the lines of bridges instead of between them. Consequently, if the finger travels along a line of red bridges, only the green strings sound:

If it travels across the green bridges, only the red strings sound:

If the strings pressing on the bridges are also set in slight vibration, this will only add harmonically to the effect. For instance the finger when passing from D to E across the bridge of the A-string may cause that string to sound slightly. The upper A is a fifth above D and a fourth above E, and the lower A is a fourth below D and a fifth below E, all these intervals being perfect ones:

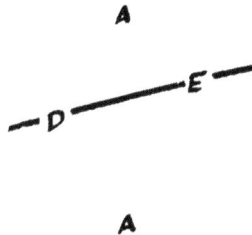

The surface of the sounding-board, under the strings, can be painted in a pattern of different colors to represent the paths of the various plures:

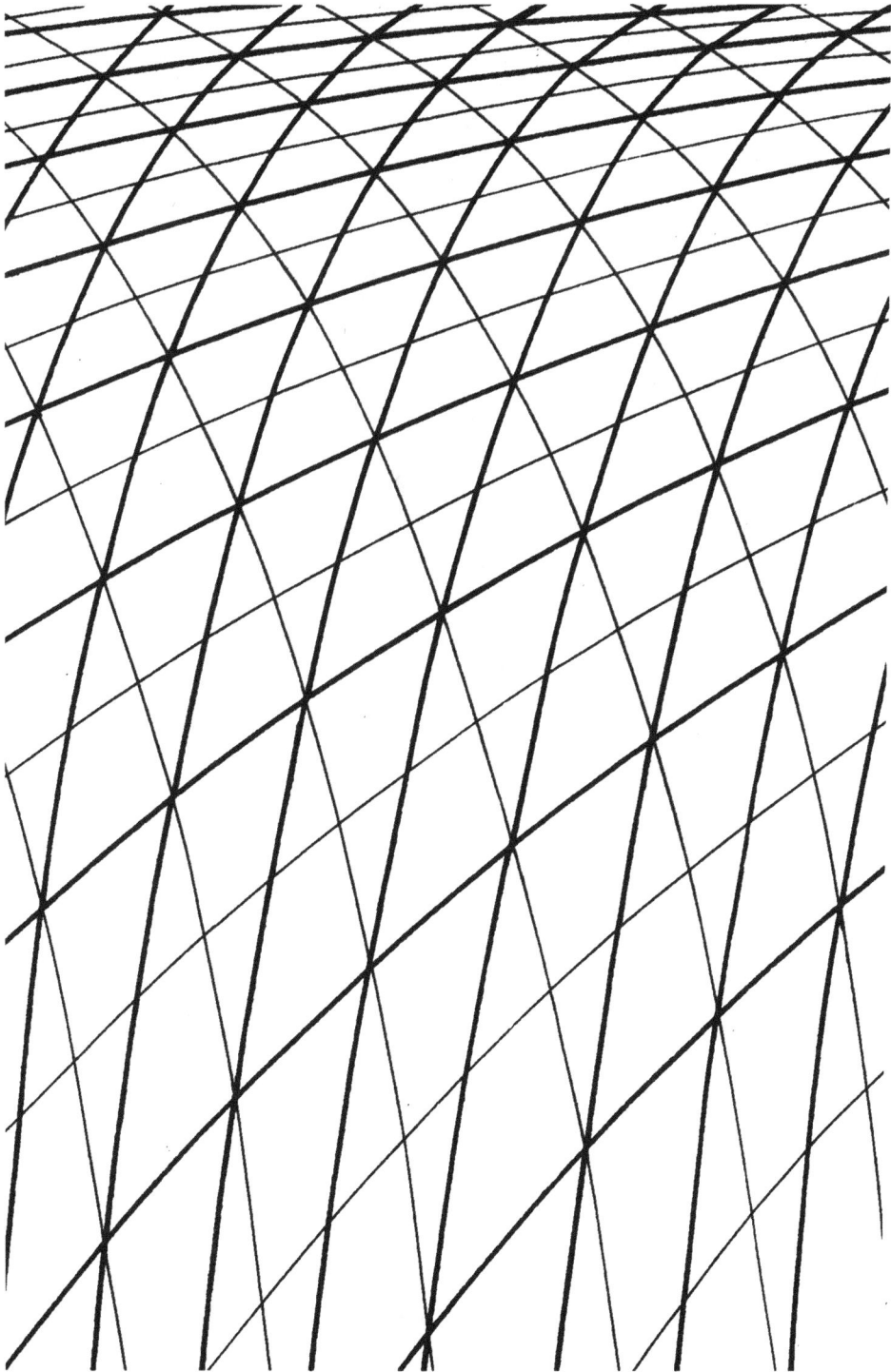

Using two fingers, the plurrier can produce *double plures*. For example, a double plure of fourths, with one finger vertically above the other, will sound in octaves:

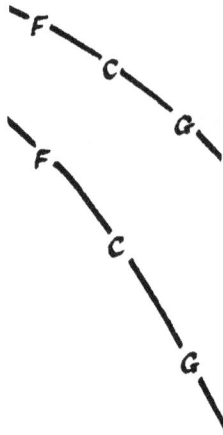

F
C
G

F
C
G

With the hand rotated a certain amount, it will sound in fifths:

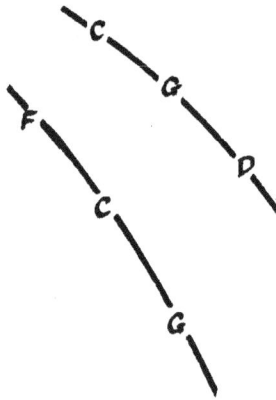

C
G
F
D
C
G

Rotated further, in seconds:

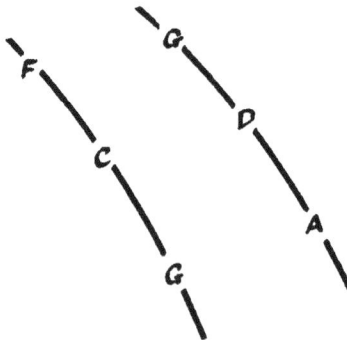

G
F
D
C
A
G

Holding the fingers wider apart, so as to strike non-adjacent sub-strings, will produce double plures in 15ths:

12ths:

9ths:

6ths:

3rds:

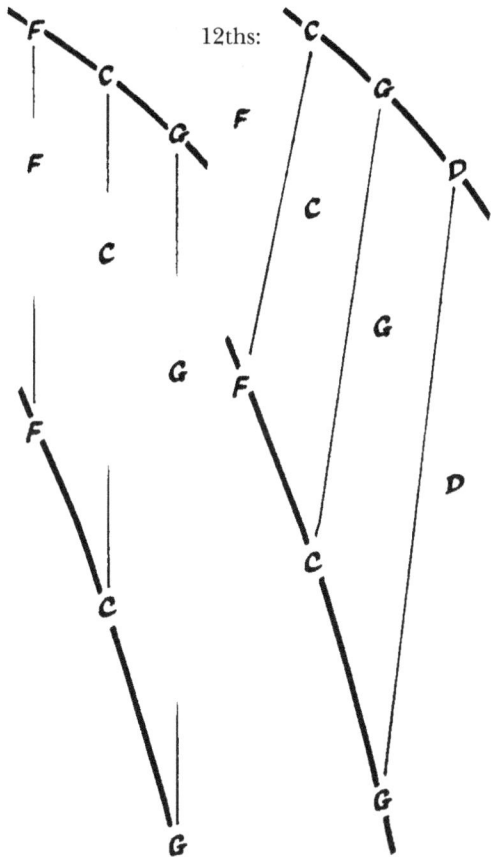

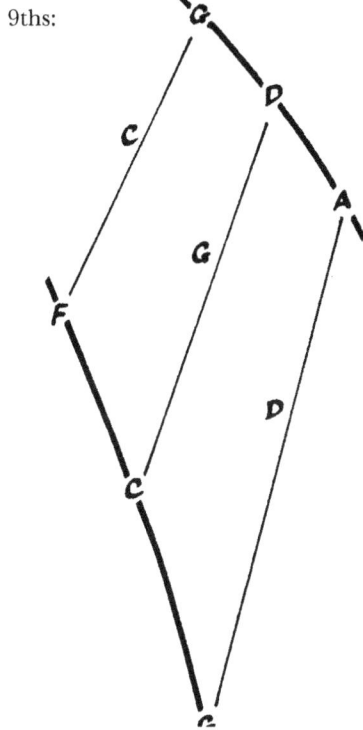

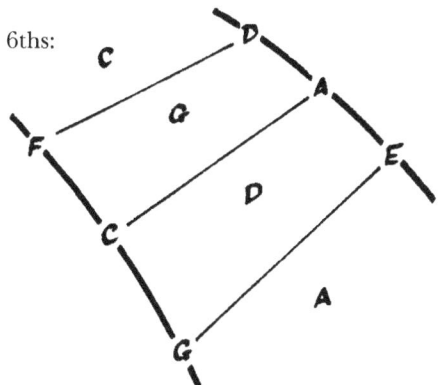

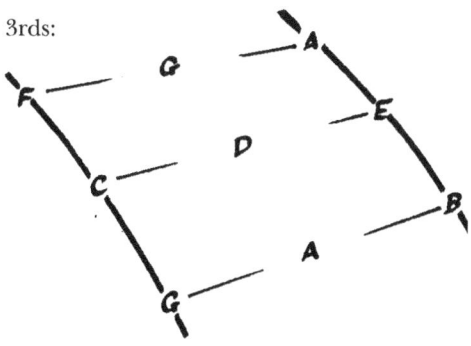

Intermediate angles of the hands will turn these into *staggered double plures*, so that the double plure of fourths in octaves becomes in effect a plure of alternate octaves and fifths:

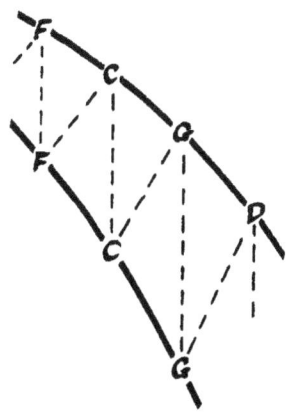

Double plures of fifths would add the harmonies of 11ths and 7ths, and double whole-step plures would of course produce all the major intervals. A double plure of fourths-and-fifths (played along both sides of a row of bridges) would produce alternate octaves and unisons (simultaneous or staggered):

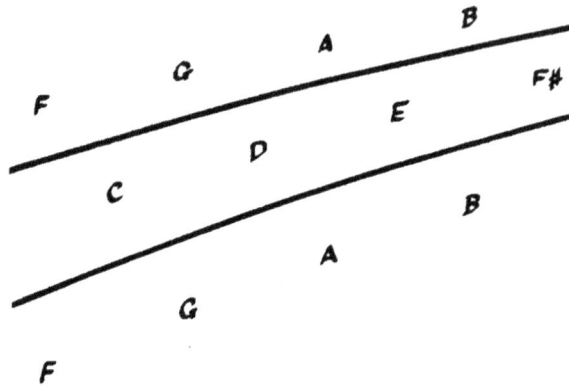

—of which the simplest (the vertical) form would sound:

```
F      G      A
     C      D
F      G      A
```

and some rotated forms would be:

```
    F              G           A
        C  C          D  D          . . .
    F              G           A
```

```
    F      G      A
    C  C   D  D                    . . .
    F      G      A
```

```
        F      G
    C              B              . . .
                   D
    F      G      A
```

—etc.

   Then there will be triple plures, and plures of various kinds played by the two hands together.

   Plures if prolonged any distance will reach out into dissonance with the tones from which they start. Further prolonged, they will run back into consonance or near-consonance, this pattern having a wave-like periodicity of twelve strings.

   Plures, unlike chords, are theoretically infinite in length, though what would actually be played would be segments of plures.

Uses of Plures

Clearly, it would be possible to play music consisting entirely of plures. This music would be neither diatonic (since it would be without tonal centers or modal patterns) nor chromatic (since it would not be confined to the circle of twelve tones) but would be enharmonic.

Ancillary to other sorts of music, plures can be used to form chords, melodies, scales, and key-transitions.

When the finger plays a tone, it—or a finger of the other hand—can be drawn away from that tone along any of at least ten radiating plure-paths:

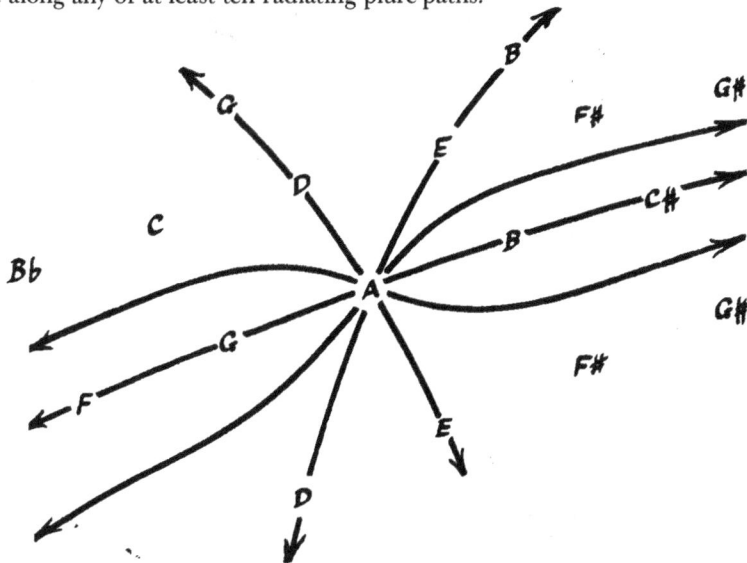

Thus a chord, or two chords, or more, may be appended to any tone in the melody. A melody could, for example, be played with alternate hands, each hand turning its own tones into chords; or one hand could be used to play the melody, the other to derive chords from it. Harmonic color would alter with the direction of the plures being used for chords.

Fourth-fifth plures, and staggered double plures, are already almost in the nature of melodies. True melodies may be formed by combining segments of plures into geometric shapes. For example, a triangle made out of a fifth-plure, a fourth-plure, and a whole-step plure:

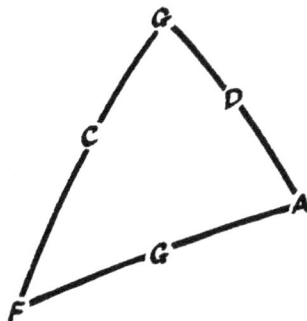

Transformations of melodies may be obtained by playing them in the opposite direction or starting from different points. In fact, a plan of the shape on the plurry would be more general than any other form in which the melody could be stated. The plan above represents a family of 6 (starting-points) × 2 (directions) × 6 (tonics) = 72 melodies, not counting time-values. Leaving the letters out would make it more general still.

However, any patterns, whether or not plure-based or geometric or passing across the centers of strings, will produce random melodies. The swirling figures that on the harp remain only visually two-dimensional will on the plurry become audibly so as well.

The scales of keys and modes are formed from segments of whole-step plures. For example the scale of C major consists of a segment of 3 out of the red whole-step plure followed by a segment of 4 out of the green whole-step plure:

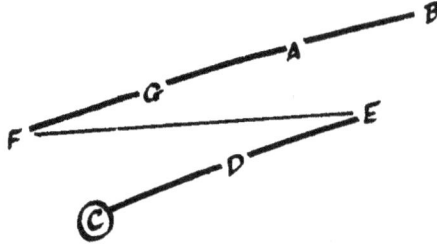

The scale of F Lydian is the same two segments in reverse order:

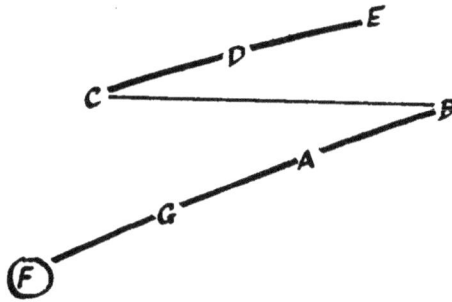

The scale of A minor consists of 2 from the green plure, 3 from the red, and 2 more from the green:

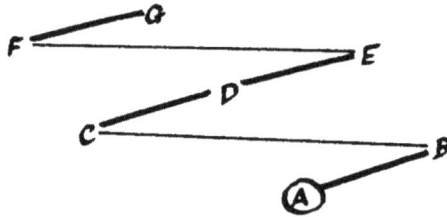

The leaps leftward-and-upward to the next plure each represent intervals of a half-step. Therefore if the plure had continued farther it would have reached a tone lying within the range of the next plure:

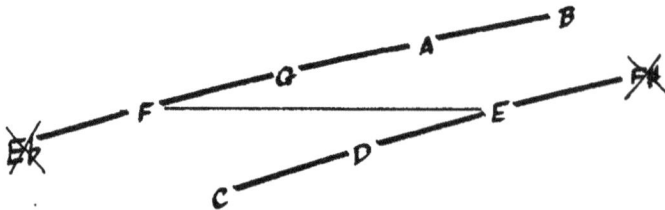

This appears as a reason why these scale-forming plures are never more than three or four tones in length.

Sets

The scale-forming plures are in fact *all* three or four tones in length, if the position of the tonic is disregarded. The A minor scale, for example, taken over a different compass, appears like this:

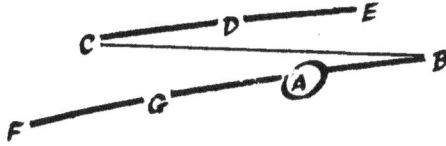

Thus all three scales—C major, F Lydian, and A minor—can be shown on one diagram by marking their tonal centers:

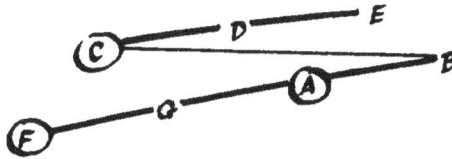

In fact the same seven strings with the other members used as tonal center will constitute the scales of G Mixolydian, B Locrian, D Dorian, and E Phrygian. We may say that these seven keys-in-modes use the same *set* of seven strings on the plurry.*

The fact is just as clear on the piano, where these seven keys-in-modes all use the white notes. What is not visually clear on the piano is that, for example, A Lydian, B Mixolydian, C♯ minor, D♯ Locrian, E major, F♯ Dorian and G♯ Phrygian also share a set. On the plurry they appear in exactly the same relationship:

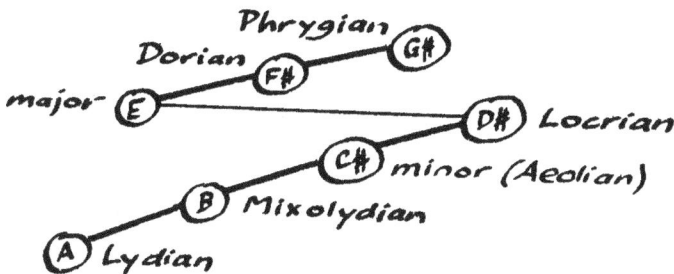

---

* Musical *modes* are orders of intervals within the scale. The modes chiefly used in European mediaeval church music were called Dorian, Phrygian, Lydian, and Mixolydian, though they had no real connection with ancient Greek music. Two others which already flourished in popular music, Aeolian and Ionian (sometimes called the *modus lascivus*), were recognized by Glareanus in 1547. Locrian, the strangest, was named but still rejected for use. Aeolian and especially Ionian practically ousted the others, and became known as the minor and major. All these "church modes" are defined by differing order of the 3 whole-tone and 2 semitone steps (the diatonic scale). In other cultures there are modes built of other (often smaller) intervals.

Set is apparently something more basic than either key or mode. A melody may, for instance, appear to be in G major and yet come to an end on E; or one half of a melody may be in minor (at any rate in the way it ends) and the other in major; or the final tone may be sometimes G and sometimes E, at the will of composer or performer. If we cannot decide whether the tonal center is G or E—and to decide on one or the other may be artificial—then we cannot say whether the mode is major or minor. But we can say that the set is the C-set: the seven tones of which, on the plurry, C is the leftmost. And this is all that we commit ourselves to in writing music on a stave, for the so-called key signatures in fact specify not keys but sets. The signature of one sharp does not really specify G major, for it may also specify E minor, A Dorian, etc.: what it really specifies is the C-set (C G D A E B F♯), within which music may be major or minor or neither.

A set is the selection of tones among which, at any one time, the musician is choosing. Out of the line (infinite number of points) of possible tones, an infinite set at a certain spacing is in use at one time:

—later another:

The plurry is a device which collects each such set of points together, so that they are not separated by points not belonging to the set. Yet all the intervening points are also present—at least, all would be if the pattern of strings were extended indefinitely to right and left. Then, too, *every* such set of points would be collected together in its own place.

Such a set appears as something visually simple and constant: seven adjacent strings (three red and four greeen, or three green and four red). The scattering of points along a horizontal line is converted into a vertical block or band up and down the board.

Another way of stating the fundamental difference in the plurry is this: Whereas in other instruments a tone is placed next to those tones nearest to it in *pitch*, in the plurry it is placed next to those tones most nearly related to it (related, that is, mathematically, musically, harmonically). In fact, it is placed farthest from those nearest to it in pitch—and almost-infinitely far from those almost-infinitely near to it.

Since a string includes all octaves of a tone, the act of selection does not have to be made anew in each octave. The sharp-sign does not have to be written on F in each stave, as it were: the F string is far away from the F♯ string, so the player does not have to remember to sharpen F each time he comes to it.

All the scales appear as paths spiraling up and down the board within a set:

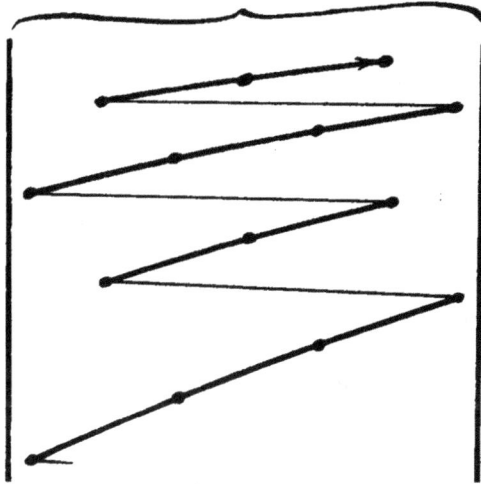

—or as all the red and green diagonal lines of bridges across the set:

We may name a set by its leftmost string. The F set is F C G D A E B (the white keys on a piano). The C set is C G D A E B F♯. The B♭ set is B♭ F C G D A E. And so on. The F set may also be called the set of naturals; the F♯ set the set of sharps; F♭ set the set of flats; F𝄪 set the set of double sharps; etc.

Statements about keys and modes may all be made in a more general form in terms of sets and strings. For example:

—More particular statements: C major is the F set with second string as center; F♯ major is the B set with second string as center. More general statement: the major mode is any set with second string as center.

—More particular statements: C major is the F set with C as center; C minor is the A♭ set with C as center. More general statement: a key of C is any set with C as center.

The plurry acts as a tabulation and reminder of keys and modes. The major mode is any set that looks like this on the plurry (the string shown thicker being the one in use as tonal center):

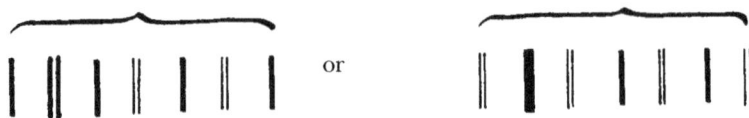

And the minor mode is any set of which the fifth string is the tonal center.

To remind yourself of which tones are used in D♯ minor, you look at the plurry (or a diagram of it) and read them off as the seven strings of which D♯ is the fifth: B F♯ C♯ G♯ D♯ A♯ E♯.

To remind yourself of what the signature of four sharps stands for, you look for the set on the plurry which lies with four of its strings in the zone of sharps and three in that of naturals: it is the A set (which may be E major, C♯ minor, etc.).

To transpose a score, you read it onto a different set but otherwise with the same relationships. Thus if a piece of music is written in G major, and you wish to play it in F♯ major instead, you move your hands five strings to the right, but then play with the same motions.

A plurry at hand would be of considerable help to anyone writing music, writing about music, talking about music, or thinking about music.

The pattern of playing

The plurry makes playing in every key and mode precisely as easy as playing in C major.

Admittedly, no set is as easy to play in as C major is on the piano, since there is the initial difficulty that the scale of one octave is not arranged in one row. However, once the player has acquired the habits necessary to master this, he can apply them without change to any other set, no matter how many sharps, flats, double sharps it may contain.

On the piano every set has a different pattern of white and black keys, which must be mastered individually. A pianist playing on the white notes only is in little danger of hitting an accidental (a tone outside the set being used) without meaning to, since all the accidentals are black and are raised and placed backward; but when he plays in E major, which is a mixture of black and white notes, he needs long training to avoid hitting the wrong ones. But a plurrier cannot hit a string outside the set he is using—whatever it is—as long as he stays inside the two parallel lines that bound the set. There *are* no unwanted strings within the set. Within each octave on the piano, there are always five tones that you want to avoid besides the seven tones that you are using. In C major and A minor the unwanted tones are clearly marked off by being black; but in all other major and minor scales, the unwanted tones are both black and white and so are the wanted ones. On the plurry, the unwanted tones simply lie away to the left and right of the set of wanted ones.

It may be that even the simple linearity of the piano C major is essentially less easy to move about in than the plurry set. Selecting tones out of a line is a matter of counting and of being careful not to hit the other tones which lie in the way: to jump from C to C you perform a rapid act of counting seven identical-looking white keys, to jump from C to G you count four.

On the plurry, to jump from C to C you move one place straight up the same string; to jump from C to G you move one place along a line at a certain angle. To jump from C to A you move along a line at a certain flatter angle; to D, at a flatter angle still; to F, in a different direction (left instead of right). Continuing along any of these radiating lines, you keep finding tones at the same interval. The act of moving at a certain *angle*—instead of a certain distance—would come to be associated in the player's muscular memory with a certain type of musical interval:

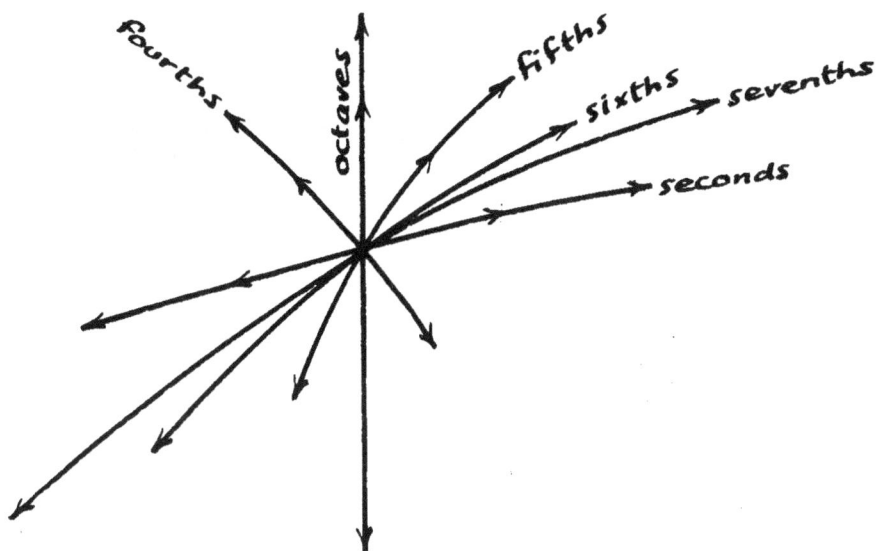

Within the set, these angular positions in which the seven sub-strings lie would come to symbolize to the player their various characters in the scale:

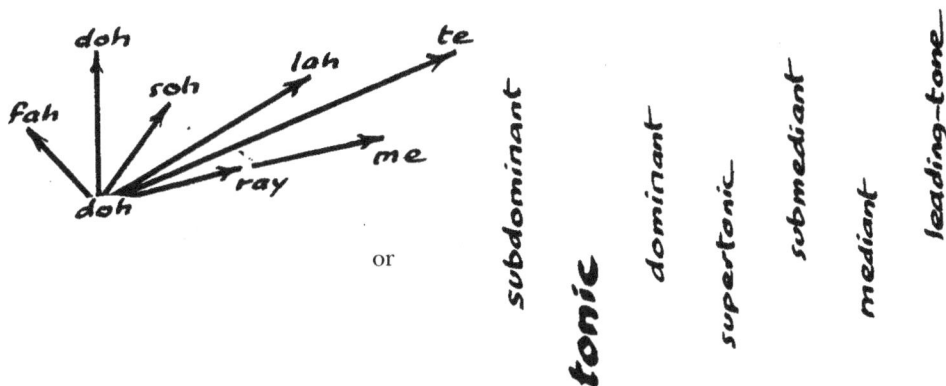

or

These are rather like the differing moves which give knight, pawn, bishop their characters in chess.

A plurrier has no need to practise scales for each key. When he has learnt the scale for one, he has learnt the scales for them all.

Here is the shape of the scale of C major on piano and plurry:

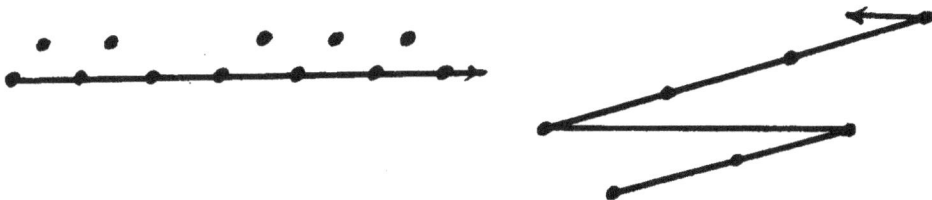

The piano scale (on the left) seems much simpler. p the tones that are avoided, in this case merely the black keys. But here is the scale of D major on piano and plurry:

20

And E major:

The pattern for every other scale on the piano is different again:

F major

G major

A major

B major

C♯/D♭ major

D♯/E♭ major

F♯/G♭ major

G♯/A♭ major

A♯/B♭ major

—while the pattern for all these on the plurry remains the same.

Fingering, even, may be more practicable, after the first stages; when the basic dexterity is learned, it may be possible to play sequences and combinations of tones that are physically not reachable on the piano. On the piano a scale of eight notes, for instance, must be fitted to the five fingers by making them leap past each other: 1 2 3 1 2 3 4 5. And of course this has to be done much more when playing sequences over wider ranges, all of which are continuations of the one line of tones to right or left. But on the plurry they are not, at least when playing diatonic music: all scales and leaps remain confined to the band of seven adjacent strings. Probably many stepwise sequences of tones would be played by one finger instead of a succession of fingers. In other cases, for instance when playing a succession like C G C´ (the second C being an octave above the first), the finger that played the first tone would also play the third, but without having to cross over the finger that played the tone between.

A kind of unskilled improvisation becomes easier. On the piano a child, for instance, can keep hitting white notes, and, whatever the demerits of his tune, at least it does not wander outside the key of C major (strictly, the F set). But this is the only set he can do it for, and if he hits any black notes they are likely to belong to distant keys. A plurrier similarly can improvise by plucking randomly among the seven neighboring strings of the F set. But he can do the same with the E set, the F♯ set, or any other. That is, a child can pick at the strings of B major or C♯ major just as strictly, if meaninglessly, as those of C major. And if while doing so he misses his aim and starts using the next string either to the right or the left, he has only shifted to either of the most nearly related keys.

Shifts

The strings to right and left of the set in use represent the tonal regions outside the musician's present purview. Into them he makes occasional excursions for an accidental; and into them also may run the chords formed by plures starting from within the set:

Persistent plures out in one direction may prepare for or constitute a transition. A change of key is a shifting of the whole set:

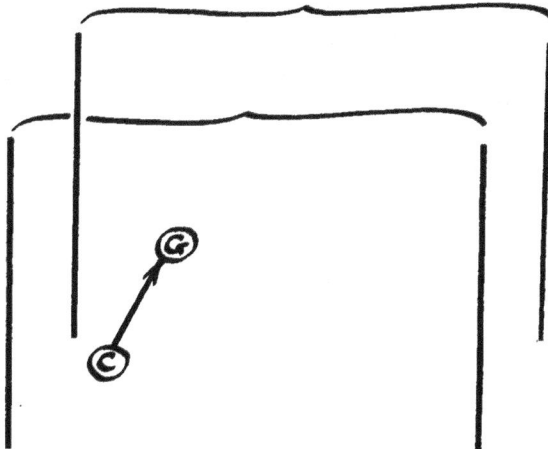

A change of mode is a shifting of the center within the set:

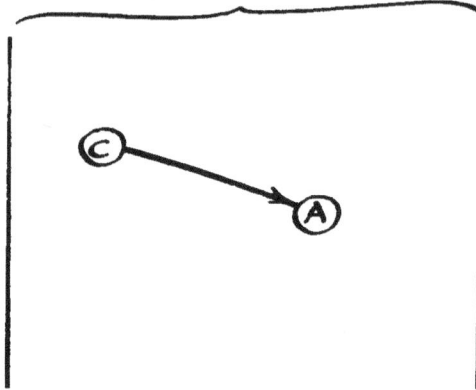

Besides 7-string sets, traditional Western music includes 6-string and 5-string sets. The hexatonic modes are sets of 6 adjacent strings with the tonal center in the 1st (Lydian-Ionian mode), 2nd (Ionian-Mixolydian), 3rd (Mixolydian-Dorian), 4th (Dorian-Aeolian), 5th (Aeolian-Phrygian), or 6th (Phrygian-Locrian). The pentatonic modes are sets of 5 adjacent strings with the tonal center in the 1st (Lydian-Ionian-Mixolydian), 2nd (Ionian-Mixolydian-Dorian), 3rd (Mixolydian-Dorian-Aeolian), 4th (Dorian-Aeolian-Phrygian), or 5th (Aeolian-Phrygian-Locrian). Thus, to re-express the diagram of mode-relations given in Bronson's *Traditional Tunes of the Child Ballads*: a melody in the major (Ionian) could by losing its left-most string pass into the hexatonic Lydian-Ionian; then, by gaining a new string on its right edge, it could pass into the heptatonic Lydian.

Hexatonic and pentatonic scales contain gaps when played on the white notes of the piano; in fact they are sometimes referred to as the "gapped" scales. But they contain no gaps when played on the strings of the plurry. Instead, the set has simply shrunk. One may say that it is psychologically unlikely for gaps in the middle of a set, or scale, to persist unfilled. All the hexatonic and pentatonic scales appear on the plurry as 7-string sets which have had one or two strings at their edges, not in their middles, omitted. In this way the plurry apparently reflects more soundly the underlying structure of the music.

Though the build of the plurry helps to show why the traditional sets of Western music are 7-stringed, 6-stringed or 5-stringed and are without discontinuities, it also, by revealing the existing situation so clearly, suggests possibilities for escaping from it. There is no reason why we should not derive new sets by omitting strings in the middle, or reducing the number of strings to 4 or 3,* or adding strings outside the 7. Thus if to C major we add the next string to the right, it would be F♯: this is the tritone, or half-octave, avoided as a dissonance in traditional harmony, but, falling between F and G, the subdominant and dominant, it would set up an interesting polarity between the tonics at the ends and the three "dominants" in the middle of the scale. Another kind of 8-string set, actually found in certain music, has an added string to the left: a melody in C major, for instance, in which B♭ is frequently used.**

---

* Bugle calls are confined to what appears to be a set of 3: C, G, C, E, G. But these are really the harmonics (multiples) 2, 3, 4, 5, 6 of a fundamental C. In other words the ratio C:E is not 192:243 but 192:240 = 4:5.

** In Germany, our B♭ is called B, and our B is called H. Hence the musical use of Bach's name by himself and by later composers paying homage to him (B A C H = B♭ A C B).

12-tone music is really that in which the set has been extended by 5 strings so that it stretches for example from F to A♯. The whole-step plures of which its scale is composed now overlap for their whole length—for half their length with the plure below, and for the other half with the plure above—and the reason for stopping at a 12-string width appears to be that after that the plures would start to overlap trebly.

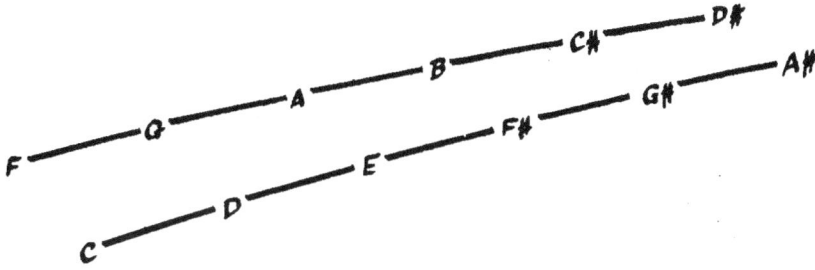

A further possibility is music with 6 whole-steps, instead of 12 half-steps, to the octave. This is obtained by omitting every second string from the set: that is, by forming a scale of only the green plure (or only the red).

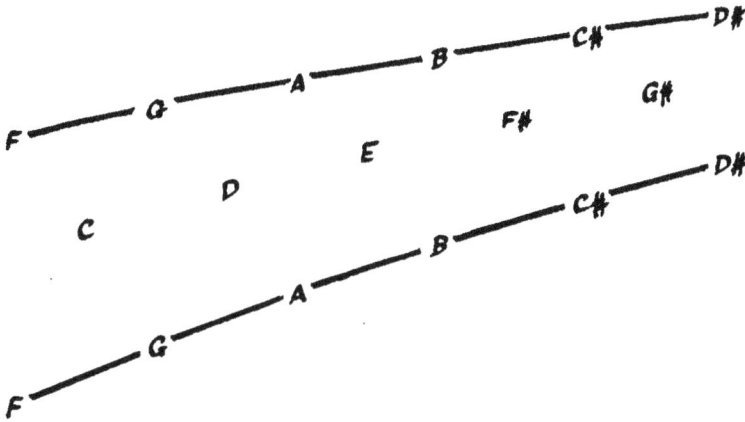

Theory

The plurry is, literally, a musical diagram materializing as an instrument:

2097152 F
1572864 C
1048576 F
524288 F
262144 F 221184 D 248832 E 1594323 B
196608 C 165888 A 186624 B 209952 C# 236196 D# 531441 E#
147456 G 139968 F# 157464 G# 177147 A#
131072 F
65536 F 59049 D#
32768 F
16384 F 19683 G#
8192 F
6561 C#
4096 F
2048 F 2187 F#
1024 F 864 D 972 E
768 C 648 A 729 B
512 F 576 G 486 E
384 C 432 D
256 F 288 G 324 A 243 E
192 C 216 D
128 F 144 G 162 A
96 C 108 D
64 F 72 G 81 A
48 C 54 D
32 F 36 G 27 D
24 C
16 F 18 G
12 C
8 F 9 G
6 C
4 F
3 C
2 F
1 F

1 represents a fundamental tone, vibrating at a frequency of 1 cycle per x of time. For example if x is $1/55$ of a second the tone is an A; or if x is $1/87$ of a second the tone is an F.*

The simplest way to derive further tones from the fundamental is to multiply its frequency by the simplest factor, 2. An octave up from 1 is 2, an octave up from 2 is 4, and so on. By these numbers we now mean relative frequency, that is, frequency relative to the fundamental: "4" is short for "frequency of 4 cycles per x of time."

Octaves being the most closely related to each other are felt to be manifestations of the same tone and are called by the same letter-name: if 1 is F, so are 2, 4, 8, 16 . . . Octaves (intervals between tones in the proportion 1:2) lie up the vertical axis of the diagram.

The next simplest way to derive further tones is to multiply by 3. Twelfths (intervals between tones in the proportion 1:3) lie along the diagonal axis.**

The doubling series alone gives us only one tone in each octave, which would be only about eight in the whole musical range; all the F's, for example, if the fundamental is an F. The second process, the trebling series, gives us every other tone there is—an infinite number of tones, in fact—but each in only one manifestation. The reason for this is that no power of 2 ever coincides with a power of 3 (or, indeed, a multiple of 3). Thus E$_\sharp$ is not quite the same as F, nor B$_\sharp$ as C, nor F$_{\sharp\sharp}$ as G, because one of them is the 19th octave $(2\{u13\}19\{u19\})$ of a fundamental while the other is the 12th twelfth $(3\{u13\}12\{u19\})$ of it: that is, one is 524288 in relative frequency and the other is 531441.

The two processes taken together give us all the tones we can use within every octave, and, in fact, an infinite number of tones in every octave. Since the octaves of a tone are regarded as further manifestations of the same tone, we can carry a series of octaves up (or down) from each member of the series of twelfths; thus each of these tones is represented in every octave. Thus as we move up the diagram the density of tones per octave steadily increases.

---

* Or $2/87$ of a second, or $4/87$, or $8/87$ . . . This fundamental is for the purposes of the diagram only; since we are going to be talking about tones 18 or so octaves above it, it must be far too deep for hearing—something like $32768/87$ or 1 vibration per 6 minutes!

** The doubling series and the trebling series form the axes of another and older diagram, the Platonic Lambda, so called from the Greek letter Λ:
—which summarized one of the systems of harmonious proportions for architecture.

A distinction is made between musical systems which are divisive or modal (India, the Middle East ancient and modern, the part of Greek music which was absorbed from surrounding peoples, early Christian and Byzantine, mediaeval Europe) and those which are cyclic or transposing (China, Pythagorean Greek, modern Western). Divisive systems arise from taking a string and halving its length to raise its pitch an octave, and touching it at other points so as to divide this pervasive interval into other intervals. Cyclic systems arise from the "cycle of fifths"—F to C, C to G, etc.—which misses the octave altogether, and which can be more deeply called a cycle of twelfths, since the ratio of F to C is more simply expressed as 1:3 than as 2:3. Thus the terms "divisive" and "cyclic" cover a simpler antithesis: the one kind of music gives isolated importance to intervals from the doubling series (1 2 4 . . .), the other gives almost as great importance to intervals from the trebling series (1 3 9 . . .). Divisive systems favor the development of drones and modes, cyclic systems favor the development of harmony. It was the Greeks who most notably com-

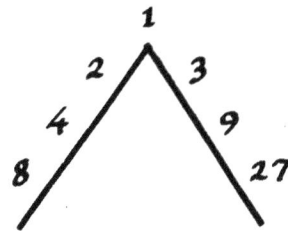

In the tenth octave (starting with the tone 512) there are 7 tones. This is the diatonic scale, the basic material of Western music at least. It can be continued upward by multiplying all its members by 2.

In the eighteenth octave (starting with 131072) there are 12 tones. This is the chromatic scale: the diatonic scale plus sharped versions of its first five members (in order of origin).

In the twentieth octave there are 13 tones, in the twenty-first 14: here the last two members of the diatonic scale are repeated in sharped versions. These (E♯ and B♯) almost coincide with the first two unsharped members (F and C): in other words, they are what is called enharmonic.

In yet higher octaves (not shown) yet more tones are added. Each is the sharped version of a tone 7 strings to the left of it, and falls only slightly higher than a tone 12 strings to the left of it. Thus there will be not only F and F♯ but also F♯♯, F♯♯♯ and so on; slightly higher than F is E♯, slightly higher than F♯ is E♯♯, and so on. The gaps between the degrees of the original seven-tone scale gradually fill up with other tones; the differences in pitch between these many tones become more and more imperceptible; yet, in theory, no two tones ever exactly coincide.*

F Lydian

The tone which the diagram leads us to use as fundamental is not C (nor A), but F. And the seven-tone scale which the diagram compels us to show as basic is not the major, but the Lydian.

If we were to choose C as the fundamental tone, then the next six tones to appear would be G D A E B F♯—not F. Only if we choose F as the fundamental will the other six tones be the other six naturals. The scale of seven naturals with F as tonic—F G A B C D E—is the Lydian scale.

It differs from the major scale in having its fourth tone raised: for instance the scale of C Lydian is C D E F♯ G A B. The untidiness that would result from taking C major as basic is shown by writing the scales of the other modes of C: C Mixolydian has one flat, C Dorian has two flats, C minor has three flats, C Phrygian has four flats, C Locrian has five flats—and C Lydian has one sharp.

* What is the significance of this anagrammatic area of the diagram?

864• 972•
  648•   729•
432•   486•
  324•
216•   243•
  162•
108•
  81•

The Lydian has to be the starting point in any other way of diagramming the modes: for instance Bronson's in *The Traditional Tunes of the Child Ballads*. The Lydian is basic (structurally, whether or not historically); the other modes are derived from it. They can be derived from it in various ways: by inversion as in chord-inversion (successively raising the bottom tone an octave or lowering the top tone an octave) or by successively flattening the tones starting from the latest in origin (B then E then A then D then G then C) or by successively taking the other tones as tonic starting from the earliest in origin (C then G etc.).

The musical staff was introduced in the tenth century as a single line representing F below middle C. It developed into our five-line staff, and the "F" with which it was marked developed into the sign of the bass clef.

Structural order—*fucigidaeb*

The order of the tones from left to right on the diagram can be called their order of origin. Or, since its repeating segment is F C G D A E B, we might mnemonically call it *fucigidaeb*. For example, in the diagram as a whole, F is the 1st in origin and D♯ the 11th. In the seven-tone scale on the diagram, F is 1st in origin and B is 7th and last. In the G set, G is 1st and C♯ is 7th. In the B♭ set, F would be 2nd.

The formula F C G D A E B is mnemonic for many other things in music. It gives the number of sharps or flats in the signature of any key, and also which sharps and flats they are:

		E♭	B♭	F	C	G	D	A	E	B	F♯	C♯	
major key	...	E♭	B♭	F	C	G	D	A	E	B	F♯	C♯	...
number of flats/sharps		3	2	1	0	1	2	3	4	5	6	7	
		B	B	B		F	F	F	F	F	F	F	
		E	E				C	C	C	C	C	C	
		A						G	G	G	G	G	
									D	D	D	D	
										A	A	A	
											E	E	
												B	
minor key	...	E♭	B♭	F	C	G	D	A	E	B	F♯	C♯	...
number of flats/sharps		6	5	4	3	2	1	0	1	2	3	4	
		B	B	B	B	B	B		F	F	F	F	
		E	E	E	E	E				C	C	C	
		A	A	A	A						G	G	
		D	D	D								D	
		G	G										
		C											

(Tables for the other modes would be identical but for the positioning of the zero under different letters—under F for the Lydian keys, etc.) The *fucigidaeb* is also the order of tones a fourth or eleventh apart (going downwards) or a fifth or twelfth apart (going upwards). (On the last of these series the diagram, and the plurry, are built.) The dominant of the key of C is G, the dominant of G is D, the dominant of D is A, and so on; going backwards, the subdominant of the key of C is F, the subdominant of F is B♭, and so on.

But within one octave the order of origin is not the order of pitch. It becomes an up-and-down order of fourths and fifths:

512 F 768 C 576 G 864 D 648 A 972 E 729 B
486 E 324 A 243 E 216 D 144 G 96 C 81 A 64 F
27 D 9 G 3 C 1 F

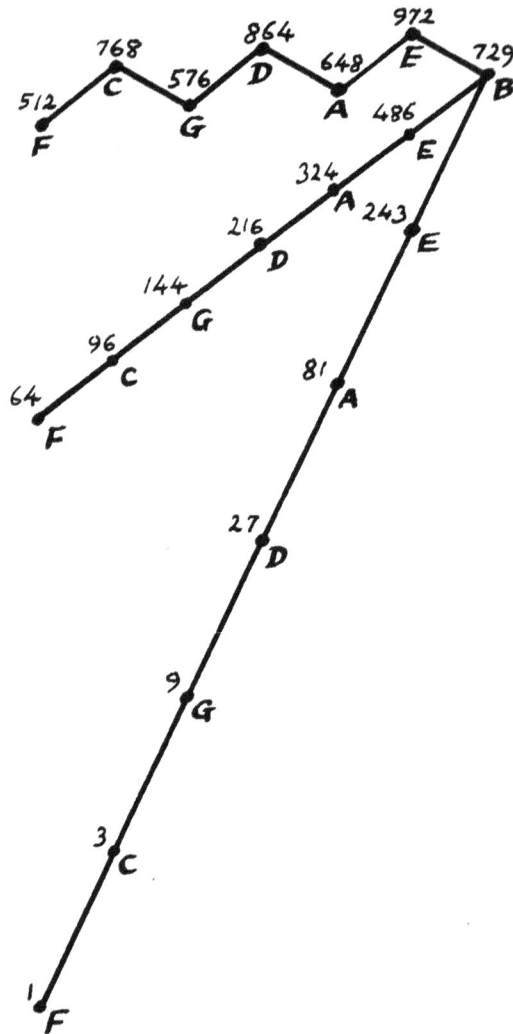

This is of course why the notion of building an instrument on such a pattern has not occurred before. On other instruments, tones are laid out in order of pitch, or, rather, order of pitch *within an octave* (F C G D A E B is also an order of pitch, but over a much greater range). Thus the diatonic scale has to be rearranged on the piano as F G A B C D E. Then, as degrees of a particular mode, they are taken in order of pitch starting from the tonic of the mode: for example F G A B C D E in Lydian, C D E F G A B in major, A B C D E F G in minor. At one time—a late stage in the fixing of the notation—the mode which we call minor, and which was then called Aeolian, was the most important. Here at last is the explanation of why the formula I have had to quote so often (F C G D A E B) is such an odd one. Instead of being named in the order of their structural origin, our tones have been named in the order of their pitch within one octave of the fifth transformation (minor) of the first seven-tone scale to be generated by the underlying laws of music.

Order of origin, like set, is a concept for which there is no previous terminology so far as I know, and which is cumbrous to talk about in terms of keys, modes, and degrees. For example, in the set of naturals, F is the 1st degree (tonic) of the Lydian mode, 4th degree (subdominant) of the major mode, 3rd degree (mediant) of the minor mode. But it is always the 1st tone in origin, or, on the plurry, 1st (leftmost) string of the set. Similarly the

5th string of the set, or 5th tone in order of origin, is 3rd degree of the Lydian mode, 6th of the major, 1st of the minor. The diagram shows what they have in common: they are always mathematically related to the fundamental tone, and hence to each other, in the same way. 1st string to 5th string is always 512:648, or 64:81.

Intervals

The musical intervals are displayed in their simplest forms in the numbers along the two axes of the diagram. Any line connecting two points represents an interval; equal parallel lines, or equal segments of one line, represent equal intervals. Thus 576:864 (G:D) is reducible to 18:27 and then to 2:3 (F:C). Here we pushed the interval down the diagram by simplifying it, dividing first as many times as possible by 2, then by 3.

An interval is expressed in its simplest form when it has been pushed as far as possible down into the angle of the diagram, so that its two ends are on the diagram's two sides or axes. And the simpler, and more important, intervals are those which are represented by shorter lines and can be pushed farther down. Here are the simplest—the perfect, major, and minor intervals:

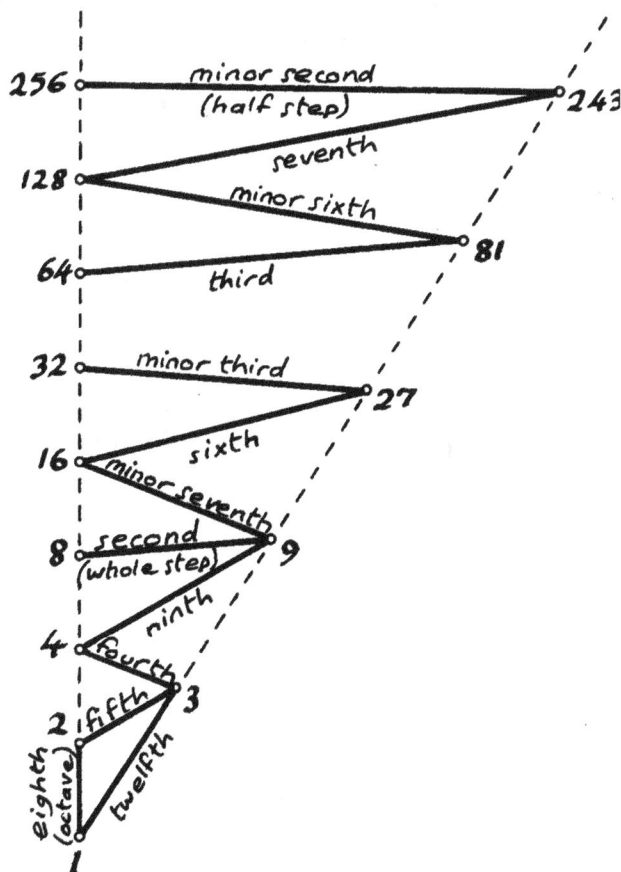

The major third, 64:81 in this Pythagorean or most natural of all natural scales, has been falsely simplified in the Zarlinian or tempered scale of our pianos to 64:80, because this is reducible to 4:5. But all other proportions are thereby disturbed; no multiple of 5 is found in the natural system.

Every ratio between numbers on the two axes of the diagram is a different interval, and every interval in the natural scale is to be found in one of these ratios.

The augmented and diminished intervals, being more complicated, are farther up the diagram. At a certain level comes the interval 524288:531441, the first enharmonic near-unison. Ratios between still larger numbers, proportionately still closer than these, represent enharmonic near-unisons which are nearer still. There is an infinity of intervals, representable by longer lines, and of decreasing importance.

The diagram shows some ways in which intervals can be classified. For instance what are called the perfect consonances—fourth, fifth, and octave, upward and downward—appear as an innermost hexagon around each tone:

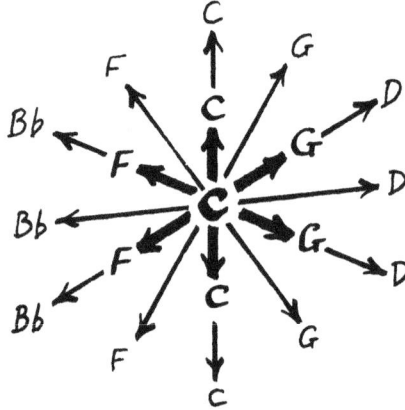

—surrounded in turn by twice as many "second hexagon" relatives at two removes, three times as many "third hexagon" relatives, and so on. It is of obvious usefulness that on the plurry a string is most closely surrounded by precisely those strings which sound most harmoniously with it.

Another function of the diagram is that from it can be read off the answers to such questions as "How many octaves do seven fifths cover?" Count from, for example, the tone 128 along the line of fifths:

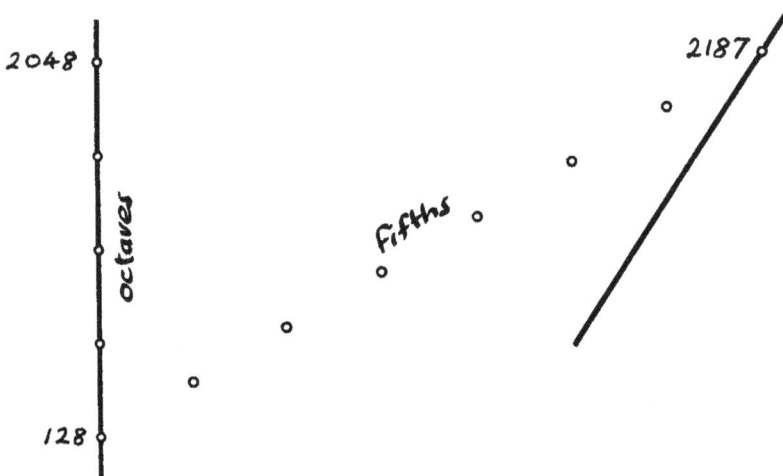

f—and you arrive at a point which is a half-step above the fourth octave. (This would be laborious and in some cases inaccurate on the piano.)

But a more important fact that can be clearly seen is this: all other intervals are mere by-products of the two basic ones out of which the diagram is constructed, the octave (1:2) and the twelfth (1:3). A fifth (2:3) is really the difference between an octave and a twelfth. A fourth (3:4) is the difference between a twelfth and two octaves. A whole-step (8:9) is the difference between 3 octaves and 2 twelfths, and a half-step (243:256) is the difference between 5 twelfths and 8 octaves. The first enharmonic near-unison (524288:531441) is the very small difference between 19 octaves and 12 twelfths.

The whole-step and half-step are generally thought of as being the basic intervals of our music, and out of them the diatonic scales of instruments are built. Now appears their highly derived nature, as compared with the intervals from which the plurry is constituted. It is because of using the truly basic intervals that the plurry is able to display so many other relationships also; whereas, though the scale of whole-steps and half-steps has its great usefulness, the cost of putting it in the foreground is that every other series is hidden.

The piano does not display the order of origin (F C G D A E B) in any form; it does not, for instance, display the series of fourths (from C to F is one kind of motion on the piano, from F to B♭ is another). Nor can it display or indeed contain the series of whole-steps or the series of half-steps (as opposed to the mixed series of whole- and half-steps), or indeed *any* series of constant intervals except octaves. For any of them, if continued, soon miss the octaves and tend away along the infinite and parallel progressions that make music two-dimensional behind the piano's one-dimensional fa\,cade.

These are some of the things about music which could be explained more easily with the help of the diagram of octaves and twelfths. Since the plurry is simply a part of the diagram which is turned into actual tones, the explainer could point to things on the diagram and meanwhile sound them on the plurry. Many he could both point to and sound on the plurry.

Transformation I: musics based on other numbers

There is one thing the diagram can show and the plurry—at least as so far envisaged—cannot. The harmonics of a fundamental tone are all its multiples (2 3 4 5 . . .). The two axes of the diagram—octaves and twelfths—consist of the first two harmonics (2 and 3) and all their powers. Therefore the diagram, however far upward it is extended, cannot contain harmonics which have factors other than 2 and 3. For instance, we have already noticed that it cannot contain the tone 5, nor 10 nor 10005 nor any other multiple of 5.

But this suggests that another axis could be drawn for any of the other prime numbers (5 7 11 13 17 . . .). The 5-axis, for example, would consist of all its powers (5 25 125 625 . . .). By adding the octaves of all these, as the octaves of the points along the 3-axis were added, a whole new area of music would be brought into existence, comparable to the traditional area between the 2- and 3-axes. All the numbers in the diagram of this music would be new ones except up the first vertical line. All the relations between tones would be new except the vertical ones. That is to say, every interval in this 2-5 music would be an interval not heard in the 2-3 music, except only for the octave. The differences between complex intervals in the two areas would become vanishingly small, but theoretically none would be identical. This would be "quintupling" music, because based on the substitution of the quintupling series for the tripling series as the means of generating new tones.

2-7 music would be septupling music; and I don't think Latin has the means to yield terms for 2-17 music and the others. Each is really a plane, intersecting with traditional music along the line of the 2-axis. In all of these, every interval, except again for the octave, would be a previously unheard one.

A further thought is that there could be music in which even the doubling series—the octaves—is replaced by another prime number. Another music would be the product of 3 and 5, another of 3 and 7, another of 3 and 11, etc.; in these the previous diagonal axis becomes the vertical axis—the pervading steps upward are twelfths instead of octaves.

Another music would be the product of 5 and 7, another of 11 and 23, another of 7 and 59 . . . : in these there would be neither octaves nor twelfths nor *any* interval used before. Each of these is a plane of numbers intersecting with 2-3 music along no line but only at the point 1. For each of these outlandish musics a new plurry could be built.

Transformation II: from natural to well-tempered scale

If on the plurry the E♯ string were in fact equal in length to the F string, and B♯ to C, as schematically shown on the drawing of the instrument, than all the strings between, also, would have to be lengthened very slightly, or lowered in pitch—those at the left least, those at the right most.

The 1:3 proportion would then nowhere be exactly maintained, but would shrink to less simple proportions like 1:2.98—each, moreover, different. The semitone or half-step intervals would shrink to become exactly half of the whole-step ones, which, in the natural scale, they are not (they are greater than half, which is why for example C♯♯ is slightly higher than D). It would no longer be useful to add further strings to right or left, for they would merely duplicate those already present: F♯♯ would exactly equal G, B♭♭ would exactly equal A, etc. In other words, the instrument would now, like the piano, be built to the tempered scale instead of the natural scale.

It is because intervals throughout have been distorted that keys in a single mode no longer sound as an identical pattern at different levels. As with the modes but more subtly, their slightly differing internal intervals have given them different moods or flavors—C major straightforward, E "moonlit," F pastoral, D minor brooding . . .

Without actually making this change, it is easy to point out on the plurry what its effects would be, and thus to explain the difference between the natural and tempered scales. To those whose visualization of music is based on the piano, this difference is hard to grasp.

Transformation III: the plurry-pattern otherwise applied

The distinctiveness of the plurry is in its arrangement. This arrangement, or plurry-pattern, need not be confined to the stringed class of the orchestra.

The generators of sound could be, for instance, bars of wood or metal, as in a xylophone. (They could be fixed in a horizontal or a tilted plane, or they could perhaps hang from each other in the form of a curtain.) In place of the bridges there would have to be gaps to allow the striker to pass from green bar to green bar without striking the red bars. The letter-names would be painted on the bars themselves. There would be an added plure: that of octaves, since the striker could run straight up a line of bars as well as across them.

Besides string-plurry and wood-plurry or bar-plurry, there could be a wind-plurry, with tubes instead of the strings, and keys to open holes halving the length of the tubes.

Finally, the plurry-pattern could be applied not to the generators of sound at all, but to a keyboard. In this case the keys, instead of varying in length, could be equally spaced as on our musical diagram. About this possibility there is more to be said.

To prescribe the relative pitches of the plurry's tones is one thing; quite another is to tune the sound-generators, so that they really have those tones. If they are wood or metal bars, and are of constant composition and cross-section, then all that is necessary is to calculate their lengths. If they are tubes containing columns of air, and are of constant cross-section, then again the problem is reduced to calculating their lengths, and the positions of the holes in them. But if they are strings, even of constant composition and thickness, it is not enough to calculate their lengths, because their tension is unlikely to remain constant. They would need frequent re-tuning; this would almost inevitably be inaccurate; and inaccuracy would destroy the pattern and purpose of the plurry.

Initially the natural scale of the plurry seems easier to tune than the tempered scale of the piano: the pitch of every sub-string is found by leaping an octave, a perfect fifth or a perfect fourth from a preceding sub-string. Judging a perfect interval (such as between two sounds vibrating at relative frequencies 2:3) is much easier to do perfectly than judging a slightly modified interval (like 2:2.98). However, every slight error in tuning a sub-string would be passed on to all following sub-strings; whereas on the piano the octaves provide a periodically recurrent correction. Tuning on the piano is essentially vertical:

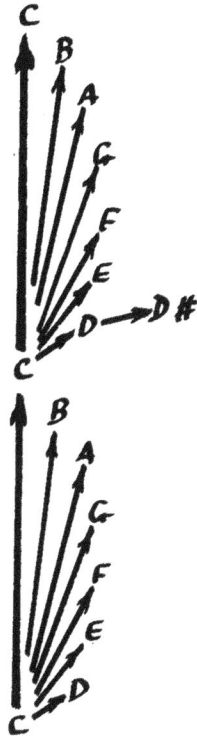

But tuning on the plurry is essentially horizontal:

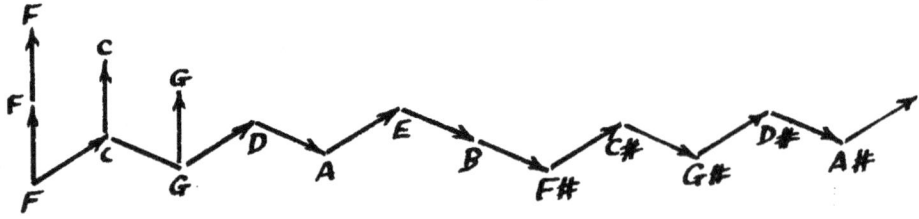

—so that most of the tones are very remotely related to the fundamental one. Yet they may be very close to it in pitch, so that the accumulated errors may easily result in a tone being just above another, or coincident with it, when it should be just below.

The solution is to calculate the exact frequency of each tone, and make a tuning fork for it, or generate it electronically and record it on tape. The calculations would be done by a computer or other machine. For instance:

$$F \times 3 \times 3 \times 3 \times 3 \times 3 \times 3 \times 3 \times 3 \times 3 \times 3 \times 3 \times 3$$
$$\div 2 \div 2 \div 2 \div 2 \div 2 \div 2 \div 2 \div 2 \div 2 \div 2 \div 2 \div 2 \div 2 = E_\sharp$$

This calculation, consisting of simple steps but many of them, is easy for a computer, though for an unaided human being laborious to the point of impossibility—especially if F represents a figure such as "347.654320987654320 . . . vibrations per second" (as it does if A is 440 vibrations per second).

When the tones have been mechanically calculated, generated, and recorded, they may be played one by one and the strings of the plurry tuned by comparison with them.

But here a further possibility suggests itself. In what order will the recorded tones be stored? In alphabetical order?—

$$A \ A\flat \ A\flat\flat \ A\flat\flat\flat \ A\sharp \ A\sharp\sharp \ A\sharp\sharp\sharp \ B \ldots$$

Or in order of pitch? This would be a complicated order such as:

$$\ldots \ G\flat\flat \ F \ E\sharp \ D\sharp\sharp\sharp \ A\flat\flat\flat \ G\flat \ F\sharp \ E\sharp\sharp \ A\flat\flat \ G \ F\sharp\sharp \ E\sharp\sharp\sharp \ ..$$

Would it not be better to store them in the same order as on the plurry? This would be a two-dimensional array, the vertical dimension representing octaves and the horizontal dimension being the order of origin:

$$\ldots \ B\flat \ F \ C \ G \ D \ A \ E \ B \ F\sharp \ldots$$
$$\ldots \ B\flat \ F \ C \ G \ D \ A \ E \ B \ F\sharp \ldots$$
$$\ldots \ B\flat \ F \ C \ G \ D \ A \ E \ B \ F\sharp \ldots$$

Then, access to these stored tones would be a two-dimensional keyboard. The rows would be bent up and down so that the keys are at heights corresponding to their relative pitches:

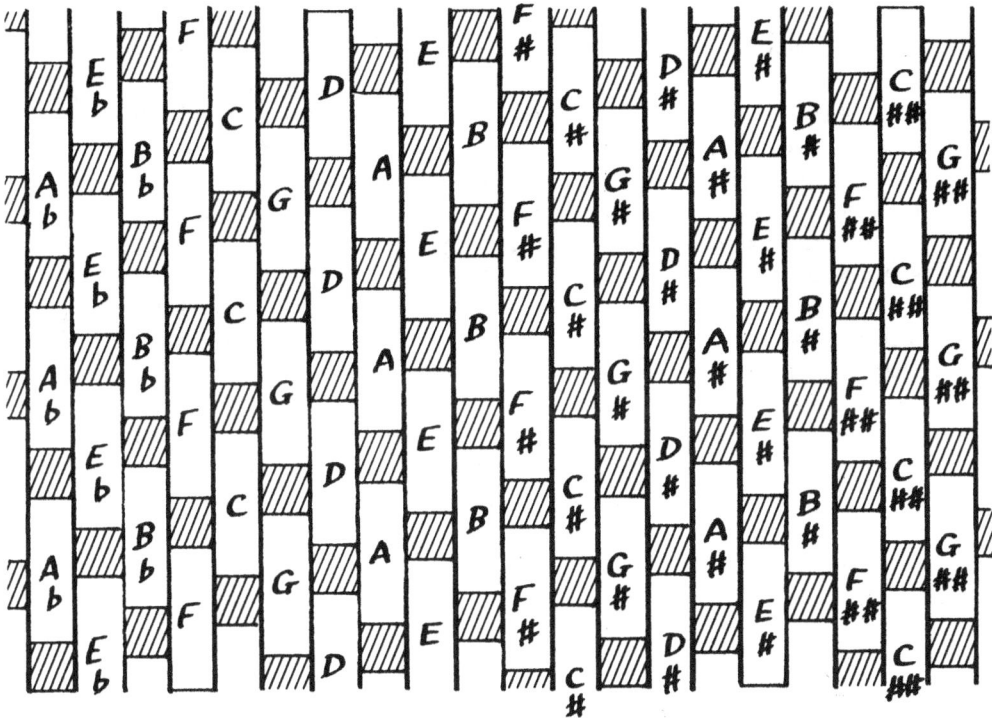

In other words, the keyboard would be on the plurry-pattern: it would be a plurry keyboard, or plurryboard, and it would operate an instrument which might be called a plurry organ.

This is probably the most realistic candidate for a plurry to be actually built.*

---

* There is one country to which this instrument is not to be imported without change of name: New Zealand, where the Maoris pronounce *bloody* as *plurry*. They might say our whole idea is *no plurry good*.

Afternote

I conceived this instrument on April 1, 1966. At least that is the date on the earliest diagram (which is essentially the same as the "Theory" graph here), and I have a lot of pencil notes from May of that year, in which the evolution of the Plurry is mixed with other ideas, with two other suggested instruments (called Diplock and Enceladon), and with influences from two musicians: Harry Partch of Sausalito (who staged ensembles consisting of such instruments as cloud-chamber bowls and soft wood marimbas played with boxing-gloves), and Akin Euba, a Nigerian composer who was my friend in Los Angeles (I had to play a bell called Agogo III in his thesis composition). The plurry was called by other names, beginning with "theory-board" and "diatonic net," and other parts of the nomenclature changed (there were such terms as *plurr, scope, stock, order of seniority, condominant series, lyde*).

(There is an instrument called "theorbo," but it is a kind of lute.)

The description was written essentially as it is here in early 1967, and there was frustrating correspondence with two musical journals then and in 1973 (when I had been encouraged by the interest of Michael Kasha of Florida State University, inventor of an improved kind of guitar). If you, reader, have generally understood this paper (and it isn't so very hard, is it?) you can compliment yourself on understanding something the Acoustical Society of America could not.

In 1998 Tim Eisele of Houghton, Michigan, made a prototype plurry. It "started as a Casio SK-1 keyboard," which he re-wired and fitted with keys in the plurry order.

He remarked: "The wiring is actually a lot more straightforward than one might think, with the output sides of the keys connected on vertical columns, and the input sides connected on more-or-less horizontal rows. I am very pleased with the way it works out. Not only is it equally convenient to play in any key, but the fingering of the chords is greatly simplified. All of the major triad chords have a single fingering pattern, with another unique pattern for all the minor triad chords. I never managed to develop the finger-memory needed to play chords on an ordinary keyboard, but it only took a matter of a few minutes with this one . . . Another nice feature is that a single hand can run smoothly all the way up and down the scale with sort of a finger-drumming motion, which I could never manage on a conventional keyboard. I have high hopes that I will be able to play this keyboard with some proficiency within a reasonable time. I believe that this key layout can make the process of learning to play a keyboard instrument considerably less frustrating."

In his photo the instrument looked like part of an interestingly tiled floor, and set me thinking of a cathedral floor that would play oratorios under walkers' feet.

www.ingramcontent.com/pod-product-compliance
Lightning Source LLC
Chambersburg PA
CBHW080535030426
42337CB00023B/4742